MW01105453

GRAMMAR'S SLAMMIN'
Code Blue – Calling All Capitals!

By: Pamela Hall
Illustrated by: Gary Currant

magic wagon

visit us at www.abdopublishing.com

Published by Magic Wagon, a division of the ABDO Group, 8000 West 78th
Street, Edina, Minnesota 55439. Copyright © 2009 by Abdo Consulting Group,
Inc. International copyrights reserved in all countries. All rights reserved. No part
of this book may be reproduced in any form without written permission from the
publisher.

Looking Glass Library™ is a trademark and logo of Magic Wagon.

Printed in the United States.

Text by Pamela Hall
Illustrations by Gary Currant
Edited by Stephanie Hedlund and Rochelle Baltzer
Interior layout and design by Neil Klinepier
Cover design by Neil Klinepier

Library of Congress Cataloging-in-Publication Data
Hall, Pamela.
  Code blue calling all capitals! / by Pamela Hall ; illustrated by Gary Currant.
      p. cm. -- (Grammar's slammin')
  Includes bibliographical references.
  ISBN 978-1-60270-614-9
  1. English language--Capitalization--Juvenile literature. I. Currant, Gary, ill. II.
Title.
  PE1450.H273 2009
  428.1--dc22
                                    2008036325

"Nurse Germ, you'll need to man the desk today," Miss Uppercase wheezed. "Please pull the capital letters—I filed them away. Proper capitalization defines people and places. The clinic won't last a minute without them."

"I can do this job with lowercase letters," Nurse Germ said as she hung up the phone. At eight o'clock, the first patient limped in.

"My name is Gus Clutz. I tripped and hurt my ankle," he gasped.

Nurse Germ's fingers flew over the keyboard.

"Hey! Who are you calling a clutz?" yelled Gus. "The capitals G and C make it mean *me*. Like that, clutz is an insult!"

"We'll fix that later," said Nurse Germ nervously. "Right now, you need to see the doctor."

But when Nurse Germ called the doctors, they had already flown the coop. The three had seen the files and said, "We deserve better than being called a pain, a droop, and a dope. We are taking the day off!"

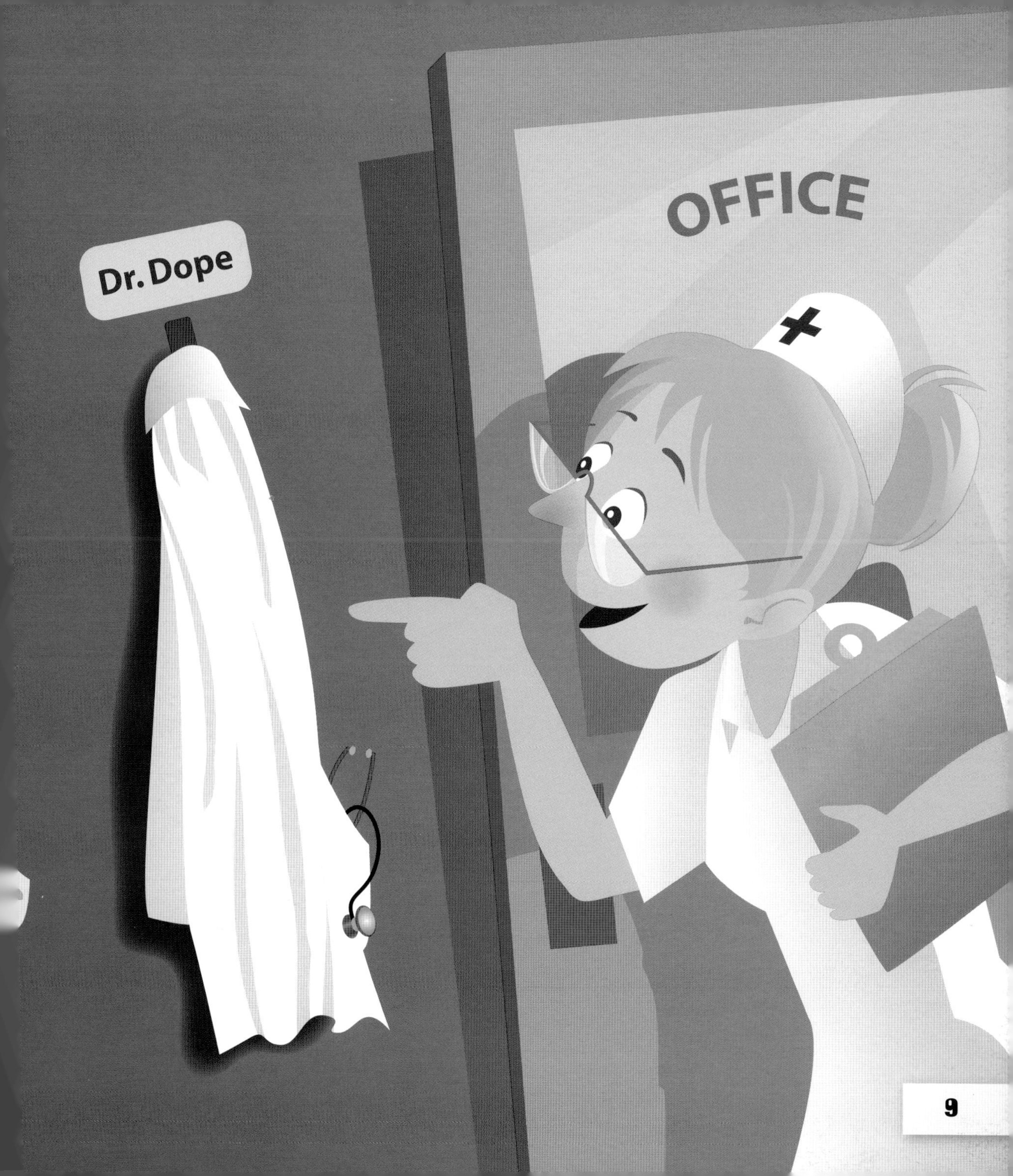
Dr. Dope
OFFICE

Nurse Germ quickly scribbled orders for Gus and sent him to X-ray. Meanwhile, the next patient filed in.

"Here's your sample," beamed Mrs. Dweeb.
    Nurse Germ grabbed the phone and dialed the delivery service. "The specimen must go out right away," she stated.

The driver couldn't believe his eyes when she handed him the paperwork.

"You must have the wrong company," he objected. "I don't work for *uds*, I work for UDS—all capital letters."

pick-up slip

delivery company:

uds

deliver to:

850 tamarack avenue

tampa florida

"Besides," he continued, "I need a street, town, and state. Proper capitalization would help this delivery go down."

"Miss Uppercase was right," Nurse Germ sighed. "This clinic doesn't work well without capital letters. Now, where would they be filed?"

She whipped through *C* for Capital, and *U* for Uppercase. But no capitals were to be found.

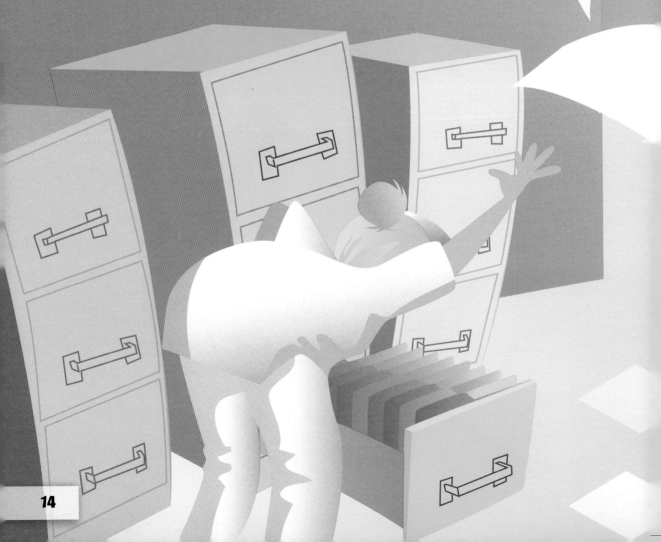

Next X-ray called, "You need capital letters to mark the beginning of each sentence. Your message to us was just one rambling note. Poor Clutz's ankle is swelling and he won't stop yelling!"

X-ray

Then Nurse Germ had an idea. She checked the calendar. It looked strange, since it said it was monday, may 5. But, she called Dr. Parr on his day off and told him about the mess.

"I see," Dr. Parr said. "This is serious, but I think I can help." He put down his putter and pulled out his notepad.

Dr. Parr passed the note to his caddy. Matt threw the golf cart in high gear. He made it to the clinic in less than ten minutes.

Nurse Germ grabbed the note and made this announcement:

"Code Blue—calling all capitals! You start sentences and give importance to proper names of patients, places, months, and days. Please come end this craze!"

Suddenly, the *R* drawer of the filing cabinet slid open with a jerk. Capital letters *A* through *Z* leaped out and got to work.

Patients were signed in with proper names. The office began working as it should.

A S p

Rr

Ss

Nurse Germ sank in a chair and made a call.
"Miss Uppercase," she gasped, "why did you file the
capitals under *R*? It's not what I expected."

"I knew you wouldn't understand," Miss Uppercase said sweetly, "but capitalization is all about *respect*."

More Notes on Capitalization

Lots of things are capitalized, including:

- The first word of a sentence
- Proper nouns, such as *Statue of Liberty*
- Names of people, places, and geographic divisions
- Names of lakes, rivers, mountains, and oceans
- Names of nationalities, tribes, and languages
- Family relationships when you are using that person's name, as in, *Aunt Donna rocks.* But not *My aunt rocks.*
- The pronoun I
- Registered trademarks and service marks
- Days of the week, months of the year, holidays, and holy days
- Even your grades are capitalized. So make sure that A in English stands big and proud!

Web Sites

To learn more about grammar, visit ABDO Group online at www.abdopublishing.com. Web sites about grammar are featured on our Book Links page. These links are routinely monitored and updated to provide the most current information available.